Alaska

Exploring America Series

Travelogue by State - Experience Both the Ordinary and Obscure

By Amber Richards

Copyright © Amber Richards 2014 All Rights Reserved. No part of this book may be reproduced without our express consent.

Table of Contents

Introduction	1
Alaska - Famous For	3
Alaska - Facts & Trivia	13
Parks in Alaska	25
Chugach Mountains	38
Ghost Towns	47
Beautiful Scenic Drives to Take	63
Special Attractions and Must-See Places to Visit	77
Annual Festivals and Fairs	105
Kid and Family Friendly Places	131
A Local's Favorite Places	141
Dangers & Safety Precautions for Alaska	145
Special Seasonal Activities	155
Public Gardens to Visit	161
Last Words of Sage Advice From a Local Resident	165

Introduction

In this series, we'll be taking a look, at one American state at a time to explore. In this book, we'll be looking at the beautiful state of Alaska.

Whether you are a resident of Alaska, or plan to visit, we'll be checking out cool places to see and interesting things to do. Some of these will be well known, popular options, while others will be more obscure, out of the way places to discover.

This was written in collaboration with a resident of Alaska, to offer a local's perspective of the area. Many times that offers a completely different view of an area, than when written by a travel guide.

The focus of this series is not so much about where to stay and eat (unless that offers a truly unique experience for the region), but about the towns, local life, nature, landscape, some history, and things to do while in Alaska.

There is also a chapter on ghost towns, popular fairs & festivals to take in, and family friendly things to do.

Thank you for downloading this book. Keep reading to enrich your experience of this amazing state!

Alaska - Famous For

Alaska, the 49th state, has many names. Alaska is the Russian version of the Aleutian word *Alakshak,* meaning 'great lands' or 'peninsula', so it is known as "The Great Land" and also as "The Last Frontier". It allows for those hardy individuals to get away from it all and retreat into the Alaska Bush.

Known alternatively at one point as "Seward's Folly" due to the fact that when Russia sold Alaska to the United States, it was thought that there was nothing there worth having. William H. Seward was Secretary of State under President Andrew Johnson and engineered the purchase. The land was sold for the price of 2.5 cents per acre. It was not until the 1890s with the discovery of gold in Alaska that attitudes began to change. Today "Seward's Day" is celebrated in

Alaska on the last Monday of March each year in honor of the purchase.

Alaska became the 49th state on January 3, 1959 and the state's motto is
 "North to the Future".

Writer and adventurer Jack London knew the lure of Alaska. So did Susan Butcher, who won the Iditarod Sled Dog race, not only once, but three years in a row and has been the only female to accomplish that to date.

Jewel, the famous pop singer, grew up in Alaska. And of course, there's Sarah Palin, the ninth governor of Alaska and 2008 Republican nominee for Vice President.

Alaska

Alaska is big – 550,000 square miles (but with only 5,000 miles of public highway). The state is so big that if you cut Alaska in half, Texas would still be the third largest state (that is, behind the two halves of Alaska). If you superimposed a map of Alaska on a map of the continental United States (to scale), Alaska would stretch from border to border (Canada and Mexico) and coast to coast. Alaska has 33,000 miles of coastline – the most of any state in the lower 48 (which, by the way, is called "outside" by Alaskans). Alaska is only 55 miles from Russia at its western-most point. Yet contrary to Sarah Palin's famous statement, you can't see Russia from her back door (in Wasilla). Alaska is simultaneously the eastern-most, northern-most and western-most state. And it borders 3 oceans – Pacific, Bering Sea, Arctic Ocean.

Even though Alaska is so large, it is the least densely populated of all the United States, with about half of the state's population living in Anchorage, Alaska's largest city. It is a mostly rural state. Most cabins are dry (no indoor plumbing, which makes it easier in the winters for the pipes not to freeze) and have outhouses. Due to its distance from the rest of the nation, it can be pricey to live here.

The state is also know for its long winters and short intense summers. However, the winters are not all bad, with the Northern Lights dancing during the clear cold nights. At Point Barrow, the summer sun does not set for 3 months. When the sun finally sets in Barrow, it is two months before it rises again. In 2013, I remember it snowing on May 17. I've seen it snow in June and August at Denali National Park. The record snow fall for a whole winter in Alaska is 972 inches in Thompson Pass about 2500 feet above sea level, north of Valdez.

Alaska

Alaska is known for its extremes – an Alaskan thermometer goes from 80 below zero to 120 degrees F. You can also go from rainforest, to tundra, to boreal forest, to the barren wastes of the Arctic, in this magnificent diverse state.

It's so large it's divided into five distinct regions – the Inside Passage in southeastern Alaska (also known as Southeast), South-central in the mountainous region, Interior in the northern section, Western in the volcanic area (or Southwest) and Northern in the northern region (the Arctic). The Bush is known as anywhere in Alaska that is wilderness.

Alaska has more mountains than buildings, more wildlife than people, more glaciers than stoplights. Alaska is home to 17 of the country's 20 highest peaks, including Mount McKinley (or, as the natives call it, Denali - the High One), the highest mountain in North America at 20,320 feet. The little town of Talkeetna is the jumping off point for the mountain climber in Alaska.

Alaska is known for its scenic beauty and abundant wildlife with large populations of bears, wolves, caribou, moose, ravens, and more, literally at your front door at times. The fishing is diverse and renowned, as well as the hunting.

Alaska

The Alaska Railroad is the only train to have flagstop service for those who live out in the bush and off the highway system. In other words, you tell the conductor where you want to get off and you can. Alaska can be reached by driving the Alaska-Canada Highway (the ALCAN), by boat, or by plane.

Alaska has the largest areas of national parklands with more than half of the parklands in the United States found in Alaska. In all, Alaska contains 322 million acres of public lands. Alaska contains 23 national parks, including 7 of America's 10 largest. Alaska has the largest state park system in the nation, which covers 3.3 million acres. It has the highest concentration of glaciers containing 100,000.

Juneau is the only U.S. capitol that can't be reached by car, by the rest of the state. It must be reached by boat or plane only (although there are roads within Juneau).

Alaska natives comprise almost 16 percent of the population and consists of 11 distinct cultures, including Athabascan, Tlingit, Haida, Eskimo, Yupik, Aleut, Inupiat, Eyak and more.

The state is also known for the Iditarod Sled Dog Race – a 1200 mile trek with a ceremonial start in Anchorage (the race begins in earnest in Willow about 100 miles north of Anchorage) to Nome. Known as "the last great race on earth", it is the most famous of the dog sled races that takes place in Alaska, where people journey from all over the world to participate. In fact, dog mushing is the state sport.

Alaska

The Gold Rush was a huge impact in the state's formation, as well as copper and silver mining. You can still gold pan here. Currently, the gold in Alaska can be accessed though the oil fields of Prudhoe Bay on the Arctic Coast. The Alaska pipeline goes through the state, routing oil to Valdez for shipping to other locations.

Alaska

The state fish is the King Salmon which can get very large. Typical weights can range from 25 - 50 pounds, but it's not too unusual to find King Salmon reaching weights in the 60-80 pound range! I can't image catching one of that caliber in size.

The state flower is the beautiful vivid blue forget-me-not. Cheerful in announcing a new season.

The state gem is jade while the state mineral is gold (what else could it be?)

The state insect is the four spot skimmer dragonfly. Contrary to popular belief, it is not the mosquito. There are at lease 25 species of mosquitoes found in Alaska. There may be as many as 40 species. They are obnoxious in the summer, along with the whitesocks and the no-see-ums. Bring plenty of insect repellant. There is a joke – the dictionary definition of "tenacious" has a picture of an Alaskan mosquito. The same dictionary for a definition of "satisfaction" has a picture of an Alaskan killing said mosquito. Another joke has to do with the mosquito being the state bird because they are so big.

The state's land mammal is the moose. Moose usually live in isolation, but at times may be seen in small herds.

The state tree is the Sitka spruce. They are the tallest conifer trees in the world.

Alaska

The ubiquitous and beautiful fireweed is unusual, in that it blooms from the bottom up. It is the Alaskan clock. When the top blooms, it signals the end of summer has arrived.

There are no snakes in Alaska. There are only a few amphibians and reptiles here – Olive Ridley sea turtle, leatherback sea turtle, loggerhead sea turtle, the green sea turtle, wood frog, Columbia spotted frog, longtoed salamander, roughskin newt, and the north western salamander.

Almost 1/3 of the state is found within the Arctic Circle, with the city of Barrow being the most northern city on the continent of North America. The supermarket in Barrow, to cope with the climate, is built on stilts so the heating doesn't melt the permafrost.

The state flag has the symbol of the North Star – the Big Dipper.

Only about one-third of Alaska is served by highways. Approximately 70 percent of the roads in Alaska are unpaved. In Anchorage, for example, there are only two highways that leave the city – one going north, the other heading south.

Alaska

There are approximately 3,000,000 lakes in Alaska and approximately 3,000 rivers.

On a clear day, Denali (Mt. McKinley) can be seen from both Anchorage and Fairbanks. The Alaska Range and the Brooks Range are the two largest mountain ranges in Alaska.

The entire state uses the same area code for telephones, except for Hyder which is 250 area code, sharing with Stewart BC and the Canadian border station near Haines.

Alaska has no plants poisonous to the touch such as poison ivy or poison oak which are found in most other states. However, it does have devil's club, which is covered with brittle yellow spines that break off easily. It is a very annoying plant and the reason why many hikers wear long pants and gloves while hiking even in the summer.

The population of Alaska is only 626,932 and compared to the population of bears in Alaska, that equals 1 bear for every 21 people. Alaska has the highest population of bears, numbering at 100,000.

Anchorage is known to be the least fashion conscious city, because here people dress for comfort and the weather. Another joke – you attended a formal event in your best clothes, your finest jewels and your Sorrels (bunny boots – which are not made out of rabbits).

And finally, I took a totally non-scientific poll on Facbook about things Alaska is known for and what comes to mind when thinking of this great state. Here are the answers I received –

Alaska

"Warm, friendly down-to-earth people who value self-sufficiency and are very resourceful!"

"Mountain men, moose, outhouses and scenic overlooks, snow and peace and quiet".

"Are not afraid of winter. As someone who grew up in MN and WI, I really love how Alaskans embrace and enjoy the cold and snow."

"Huskies, dog sled race, long nights, aurora borealis, settlers, gold mines, beautiful land, sunrise, sunset, mountains, fresh cold air."

"Pioneer spirit, beautiful creatures, not keeping up with the Jones...the Free Box [a community "thrift" store with no money exchanged for goods or materials], self-reliance, the view, you"

"To many in the Lower 48 [or "Outside"] AK is known for bears and Sarah Palin. The first two things people down here ask me when I say I lived in AK are "did you ever see a bear" and "what do you (or Alaskans) think of Sarah Palin"

"A more relaxed way of living. Hunting, fishing, camping, the big moose and her baby laying in my front yard right now and most definitely, the Northern Lights."

One more thing I'd like to add, tourists are usually surprised that we use American money and speak English too.

Parks in Alaska

Alaska has contained within its borders, 8 stunning national parks. They are: Gates of the Arctic, Katmai, Kenai Fjords, Denali, Glacier Bay, Kobuk Valley, Wrangell-St. Elias, and Lake Clark. The Kobuk Valley and Kenai Fjords are the only ones not classified as both national preserves and parks. The parks are diverse and wild, some are world famous, while others are obscure. Some of the parks are not accessible by roads at all, but can only be entered by boat, plane, or on foot.

President Carter signed the Alaska National Interest Lands Conservation Act (ANCILA) to provide for millions of acres of parkland in Alaska. The Act enabled 42,585,000 acres of parklands dedicated to Alaska. One of the most significant land conservation acts in the United States, that statute protects over one hundred million acres of land in the state.

ANILCA enlarged the park acreage in Alaska by over 43 million acres. Within that scope it created 10 new national parks and increased the size of three other parks.

Denali National Park

Denali National Park and Preserve is the one I'm most familiar with. The park contains six million acres of some of the most beautiful scenery ever imagined and is home to Mt. McKinley (Denali), North America's highest peak at 20,320 feet. The little town of Talkeetna is the jumping off point for the climbers looking to summit the mountain. Wildlife abounds in the park. There is a 90 mile road in the park but you can't drive it! Only special park buses drive the road all summer in order to preserve the wild nature of the park. Every September there is a road lottery where you can put in to drive the road for one of four days. Denali also boasts the only sled dogs in use, in the National Park Service. There are ranger led hikes throughout the park and backcountry experiences. An amazing overwhelming experience.

Wrangell-St. Elias National Park

The next park I am most familiar with is Wrangell-St. Elias National Park. . Wrangell-St. Elias National Park is huge, 13.2 million acres in scope, currently the biggest national park in the U.S. You arrive in McCarthy and visit Kennicot, a ghost town. Home to several glaciers, including the Root Glacier, which is easy to access and hike on. The most stunning moment of my visit was hiking on this glacier and drinking some of its pure water. The awesome beauty of this place just made me cry. Home to Mt. Blackburn at 16,390 feet is the fifth highest peak in the United States and twelfth highest in North America. It is also the home of my favorite mountain climbing story. Dora Keen was the first woman to mountaineer in Alaska, and made the first ascent of Mount Blackburn by going up the south side of the mountain, a route that is often avoided these days based on its difficult challenges.

Glacier Bay National Park

Glacier Bay National Park and Preserve is located north of Alaska's Inside Passage to the river called Alsek, surrounding a large saltwater bay. This is the largest protected area internationally on Earth, a whopping 25 million acres! The area offers stunning tidewater glaciers, shore lines with steep fjords, pristine lakes & rivers, and majestic mountain ranges.

Taken at Katmai National Park

Katmai National Park and Preserve is found at the top of the Alaskan Peninsula area. It was established to preserve the history of the 1912 volcanic eruptions of Novarupta and Mt. Katmai volcanoes and spans 4 million acres. It also contains the 'Valley of Ten Thousand Smokes'. It is a region filled with salmon and brown bears and is critical to provide their habitat.

A virtually untouched wilderness area is Gates of the Arctic National Park. Visitors can wander wherever they want in the 8.4 million acre park, as there are no set routes, but the terrain is challenging, so only the most seasoned outdoor enthusiasts should go there, though there are flight-seeing tours and daytrips available. There are 3 herds of caribou that migrate through the park in spring and fall. The park remains virtually unchanged except by nature.

Kenai Fjords

Kenai Fjords was created by the Alaska National Interest Lands Act of 1980. One of the most prominent features of this area contain almost 40 glaciers that flow from Harding ice field. One of the best ways to explore this region is via a boat tour.

Alaska

Kobuk Valley National Park is near the Waring and the Baird range of mountains. It is a place of large caribou migration paths in both the fall and spring. There are many fossils from the ice age found in regions of this park.

Lake Clark National Park is a wilderness area, with very diverse ecosystems and regions with the area. It is located from Cook Inlet, to the tundra of the western interior, covering 4 million acres. Within this expanse is also the Chigmit Mountains. It also is home to 2 active volcanoes, Mt. Iliamna and Mt Redoubt. Lake Clark itself is a vital salmon habitat and is a whopping 50 miles in length.

Alaska National Preserves are Aniakchak National Monument and Preserve, Bering Land Bridge National Preserve, Noatak National Preserve, and Yukon-Charley Rivers National Preserve.

Aniakchak is one of the most rugged and least visited places in the National Park System, due in large part to its very challenging weather conditions and remote location. This area is a visual reminder of the state's location in a volcanically active region, sometimes called the 'Ring of Fire'. This area contains a 6 mile wide, 2,500 ft deep bowl in the earth, made by a huge volcanic eruption over three thousand years ago. Vent Mountain is more accurately a volcano located within another volcano. There is a large brown bear population in this area. Aniakchak is not accessible by road, so to reach it a person must either use a boat or plane to get there.

Found on the northwestern side of Alaska, the Bering Land Bridge National Preserve on Seward Peninsula, was an ancient connection of land between Asia and North America. Many scientists concur that it was this crossing (Beringia) that many people groups first passed to the Americas from Asian regions. No roads lead into the actual preserve.

Noatak National Preserve holds the Noatak River, which is a wild rushing, scenic river. It's a popular location for wilderness float trips, and other rafting opportunities, from the Brooks range area to tidewaters of Chukchi Sea. The river has an intact, unaltered ecosystem. About 90% of Noatak National Preserve is wilderness, making it the 4th largest wilderness in the United States. You'll find no roads, no trails, no campgrounds within the preserve. In fact, the park's headquarters & visitor center are located in Kotzebue, an airplane ride away.

Four national parks in western Alaska are managed by one park superintendent and staff that makes up an area commonly called

Western Arctic National Parklands, and are managed from Kotzebue. The area comprises; Noatak National Preserve, Kobuk Valley National Park, Bering Land Bridge National Preserve, and Cape Krusentern National Monument.

The Bering Land Bridge National Preserve has their offices in Nome.

Alaska

Yukon-Charley Rivers National Preserve is home to the beautiful Yukon River and the Charley River basin. In the Charley River a person is permitted to pan for gold, but must use only a spoon and a pan. This watershed is a whopping 1.1 million acres and is managed by the government.

Alaska's national monuments include Cape Krusenstern and Aniakchak National Monuments.

Cape Krusentern is located north of the Arctic Circle and contains seventy miles of coastal shore on the Chucki Sea. The large area is home to shorebirds from even as far south as South America.

Chugach Mountains

The United State's first and second biggest national forests are the Tongass (which is 17 million acres), and Chugach (5.6 million acres), located in southern Alaska. The mountains protect the more temperate rain forests and coastal mountains in the region.

Alaska

The Arctic National Wildlife Refuge (ANWR) is located in the northeast corner of the state and is a large 19 million acres in scope. If this region were a state, it would be bigger than ten other states in the lower 48. It is found north of the Arctic Circle and over a thousand miles south of the North Pole.

Educational parks like Sitka and Klondike Gold Rush teach guests some of the state's history from a human standpoint, of various indigenous traditions to the history of Alaska's mining.

For example, the Aleutian World War II National historic area, preserves the memory of the only American soil occupied in the war. During World War II, the remote Aleutian Islands, home to the Aleut people for over 8,000 years, was an intense battleground in the Pacific. This area experienced a fifteen month war by air with Japanese forces and was among the battles with the highest casualties in the Pacific Theatre.

In the same vein, Kiska Battlefield is protected by the National Park Service. During World War II, Japanese forces occupied Kiska and other Aleutian Islands. As described above, it was a fiercely contested battle. The campaign ended with the recapture of Kiska Island. Even though Kiska Battlefield is in a remote location, it's threatened by erosion, looting and decay. In 2009, the National Park Service's Alaska Regional Office, in partnership with U.S. Fish and Wildlife Services was awarded an American Battlefield Protection Program Battlefield grant to conduct a cultural landscape survey of the battlefield.

Alaska

Klondike Gold Rush National Historic Park commemorates the Klondike Gold Rush started in 1897 by protecting the trails, historic boomtowns and buildings of the Klondike Gold Rush Era. In fact, in 1998, the international significance of the Klondike Gold Rush was officially recognized by Canada and the United States with the creation of the Klondike Gold Rush International Historical Park. The site in Skagway, Alaska represents the "Gateway to the Klondike". Other locations making up the international park include sites in Seattle WA, and a Canadian Park including Chilkoot Trail National Historic Site and Dawson Historical Complex National Historic Site.

A battle site is found at the Sitka National Historical park that preserves the history of this battle that was between indigenous people and invading Russians. Visitors are made aware of Russia's colonial legacy in North America, that is not commonly known about.

Sanctuaries, wildlife reserves and refuges are many in Alaska and offer incredible viewing opportunities. Here are some to check out: Walrus Island game sanctuary, Susitna Flats game refuge, Stanprice wildlife sanctuary, Sheep Mountain viewing, Anchorage Coastal wildlife refuge, McNeil River sanctuary, Palmer Hay Flats refuge, Redoubt Bay Critical Habitat area, Minto Flats refuge, Chilkat Bald Eagle preserve, Dude Creek habitat area, Goose Bay State Game refuge, Mendenahll Wetlands refuge, Pack Creek Brown Bear viewing, Creamer's Field migratory waterfowl refuge, and Delta Junction state bison range. These are all incredible places to visit for photographers, artists, nature enthusiasts, and bird watchers.

Alaska

In addition to all this, Alaska has 119 state parks spread across Southeast, Southcentral, Interior and Western Alaska. These include Afognak Island Park, Anchor River Recreation Area, Baranaof Castle hill historic site, Bettles Bay Marine Park, Big Bear/Baby Bear Marine Park, Big Delta Historical Park, Birch Lake Recreational Site, Boswell Bay Marine Park, Buskin River Recreational Site, Caines Head Recreational Area, Canoe Passage Marine Park, Captain Cook Recreational Area, Chena River Recreational Area, Chena River Recreational Site, Chilkat Bald Eagle Preserve, Chilkat Islands Marine Park, Chilkat Park, Chilkoot Lake Recreational Area, Chugach Park, Clam Gulch Recreational Area, Clearwater Recreational Site, Crooked Creek Recreational Site, Decision Point Marine Park, Deep Creek Recreation Area, Delta Recreation Site, Denali State Park, Donnelly Creek Recreation Area, Driftwood Bay Marine Park, Eagle Trail Recreation Site, Entry Cove Marine Park,

Fielding Lake Recreation Area, Ft. Abercrombie Historical Park, Granite Bay Marine Park, Halibut Point Recreation Site, Harding Lake Recreation Area, Horseshoe Bay Marine Park, Independence Mine Historical Park, Jack Bay Marine Park, Johnson Lake Recreation Area, Kachemak Bay and Wilderness Park, Kasilof River Recreation Site, Kayak Island Marine Park, Kenai River Special Management Area, Lower Chatanika Recreation Area, Nancy Lake Recreation Area, Magoun Islands Marine Park, Wickersham Historic Site, Moon Lake Recreation Site, Mosquito Lake Recreation Site, Ninilchik Recreation Area, Old Sitka Historic Site, Pasaghak River Recreation Site, Point Bridge Park, Ziegler Cove Marine Park, Portage Cove Recreation Site, Safety Cove Marine Park, Salcha River Recreation Site, Sandspit Point Marine Park, Sealion Cove Marine Park, Security Bay Marine Park, Shoup Bay Marine Park, Shuyak Island Park, South Esther Island Marine Park, Quartz Lake Recreation Area,

Stariski Recreation Site, Sawmill Bay Marine Park, Sullivan Island Marine Park, Sunny Cove Marine Park, Surprise Cove Marine Park, Thumb Cove Marine Park, Tok River Recreation Site, Resurrection Bay Marine Park, Totem Bight Historical Park, Upper Chatanika Recreation Site, Wood-Tikchik Park, and Summit Lake Recreation Area. Whew, that'll take a lifetime to explore!

Serenity Lake in Tundra

Ghost Towns

There are many ghost towns in Alaska. Many were gold rush boomtowns or other mining towns that are now abandoned or sparsely populated. Here are a few. They can be very interesting to visit and discover the history of the locations.

Kennicott Alaska with Mount Blackburn in Background

Kennicott is the first town that comes to mind for me since it's one I have visited. In Wrangell-St. Elias National Park, it's connected with McCarthy, a town of 28 at the 2010 census. Kennicott was a copper mine and made the most money out of any mine in Alaska. Kennicott was the mine and McCarthy was the, well, party town for the mine workers. You can still see the old mines in Kennicott, and there are bits of turquoise, malachite and other minerals you can pick up. What a great trip that was, seeing the mines and walking on the Root Glacier!

Chena was a small community found in Alaska's interior region, near the Tanana & Chena rivers confluence. Its prime was the first 2 decades of the 20th century with a population of roughly 400 people in 1907. That population had dropped to 138 by 1910 and the town gradually disappeared. Today it's a suburb of Fairbanks.

Alaska

Curry is a small unincorporated community in South-central Alaska just outside of Talkeetna. Once with a beautiful hotel and a stop on the train, the community has just a few hardy souls who use the flagstop train to get in and out.

Dyea is a town mostly abandoned currently, with only a few people with small homesteads occupying the valley. Located at the convergence of Taiya Inlet and Taiya River, on the south portion of Chilkoot Pass within the Skagway Borough. During the gold rush era, gold miners would disembark at the port, and travel via the Chilkoot Trail, over the mountains to the gold fields near Dawson City, roughly five hundred miles in distance.

Iditarod is located in the Koyyukuk Yukon Census area, but now is an abandoned town when prospectors discovered gold elsewhere. The city of Iditarod was founded as a focal point for other gold fields nearby.

It rapidly became a busy boomtown. By 1930, most of the gold had been found and many of the folks moved to Flat, even taking several of the buildings as well. Only one cabin and a couple of ruins are left. It is one of the checkpoints on the path of the Iditarod dog sled races, in alternate years.

Independence Mine is a State Historical Park

Independence Mine is classified as a Historical State Park. It is actually a combination of two mines brought under the Alaska Pacific Consolidated Mining Company. At its busiest point, 22 families lived in the nearby Boomtown. In 1974, it was registered in the National Register of Historic Places. It preserves the memory of living and working in a large mining camp in Alaska. People are still allowed to pan for gold here, but only with a shovel and pan.

Ophir is found in the Koyukuk Yukon Census area. It was named after a place in the Old Testament known for its wealth. The site experienced a gold rush in 1906, and population peaked in 1910, with 122 people. It is now a ghost town, but is also a checkpoint for the Iditarod Sled Dog Race.

Cape York was a town on the coastal shores, that grew during the beach gold rush nearby, and found near Nome. Tin mines were first discovered there.

Chicken is a surviving gold rush town, one of only a few in Alaska. Its origin began as a gold rush community soon following the Klondike Rush. Prospectors moved to Chicken, but when the time came to officially give their new town a name, the popular choice was Ptarmigain, which was the state bird and resembles a chicken. Spelling Ptarmigain proved problematic, so it was decided to simply name it 'Chicken'. A U.S. post office officially opened in 1903 and is still operational, yet mail is delivered twice weekly by plane. Panning for gold is still done currently. It is very rustic however with no phones, central plumbing or electricity.

Alaska

Eagle is a town found on the Yukon river, near the Canadian border in Fairbanks Census area. By 1898 the population in the area had grown to over 1,700 people due to the Klondike gold rush. In 1901 it was incorporated, the first one in the Alaska interior area. Gradually other gold rushes drew most of the population to other areas and by 2010, the population was 86. Eagle is named for the large population of eagles in the area and the historic district is a national historic landmark. They are a checkpoint in the Yukon Quest sled dog race every year in February.

Knik is a ghost town located southwest of Wasilla. The town site is listed on the National Register of Historic Places. It served as a vital 'stock up on supplies' stop for gold miners traveling to the Susitna, Chulitna, Willow Creek, Flat, Iditarod, McKinley and Gold Creek areas. A new railroad built in 1916 from Anchorage to a construction camp called Wasilla, signaled the end of Knick's existence.

Nome - The gold rush in Nome was in 1898, and was a draw to 30,000 people. It had a fifteen mile mining camp on the shores where over a million dollars worth of gold was mined, from that beach camp in 1899. Currently, Nome is home to about 3,000 people and can only be reached by plane. It is famous for being the destination of the dog sleds known as the 'Great Race of Mercy' in 1925, where the sleds contributed largely in the transportation of diphtheria medicine in harsh conditions, where transportation is difficult.

Alaska

Skagway Alaska

Skagway was the beginning location of the Klondike Gold rush in 1896. Within 3 months, it grew from one cabin to 15,000 residents. When the rush had finished, the town dwindled to about 800 residents, which is today's population as well. The port of Skagway is a favorite stop for many cruise ships. Tourism is important to local businesses. The Yukon Route and White Pass gauge railroad, which is a portion of the mining history, currently is in operation for the tourists and operates in the summer months.

Anvil Creek – This former gold mining camp is located along the Bering Sea, northwest of Nome. The actual location is undetermined.

Chitina (pronounced Chit-na) - Copper ore was found around 1900, on the north side of the Chitina River valley. New homesteaders and miners were attracted to the area because of this. A thriving community was established by 1914, due in part to a railway system that was built. In 1938, mines in the area closed and support activities moved to the Glennallen region, making Chitina a virtual ghost town.

Chisana – In 1985, the community was listed on the National Register of Historic Places as a historic district. Chisana is the highest community in Alaska at 3,318 feet above sea level. Current population is 0.

Council was built in 1897 and 1898, when gold was discovered near Ophir Creek. Council may have had as many as 15,000 inhabitants during those years. The residents left to work larger discoveries of gold near Nome around 1900. Council has about 25 old buildings and much old mining equipment, including a dredge, laying about the area. During the summer, Council is used as a fish camp, and recreational location for residents of Nome and White Mountain to enjoy.

Flat is a census designated place in the Yukon-Koyukuk census area. As of the 2010 census the population was 0. Its post office closed in January 2004. This once booming town was also fueled by the discovery of gold. By 1914, the community had grown to about 6,000 people. However, by

1930, the population had declined to 124. No plat was filed for Flat, and the town site rests on mining claims, so the existence of Flat may contravene the law, but the U.S. Post Office acknowledged the community until 2004. Between 1986 and 2000, the primary year-round residents were a family of five, who worked together to maintain the area in the winter, for mining in the summer.

Portage is a former settlement located at Turnagain Arm, roughly forty seven miles south of Anchorage. Portage was nearly completely wiped out due to the 1964 Good Friday earthquake. The ground in this area sank almost 6 feet, making most of it below sea level. What is there now are ruins of several buildings and a dead forest. The forest died when salt water flooded their roots. Today there is only a road junction and a railroad that connects the Seward Highway to the Alaska railroad.

Tin City - the only people you'll find in this area is at the radar station that is only minimally manned, and is found in the Nome census area. It is located at the mouth of Cape Creek on the Bering Sea, on Seward Peninsula. In 1903, a mining camp was built at the base of Cape Mountain where tin ore was mined.

Kantishna is an unincorporated community in Denali Bourough within Denali National Park. Founded as a gold mining camp in 1905, it endured longer than similar communities in the area, having been constructed nearest to the source of the gold. It lies in the Kantishna Hills near Eureka Creek and Moose Creek 3 miles northwest of Wonder Lake, and near the mouth of the Kantishna River. Although the community was once also called "Eureka", the Board on Geographic Names officially ruled in favor of "Kantishna" in

1944, the name given to the post office that was built on the site in 1905.

Glitter Gulch – Many years ago the entrance to Denali National Park was rather bare – just a few hotels, and a couple of restaurants. However, the past few years have brought incredible growth, some attractive, some not so attractive to the area. So now the rather small area is filled with eateries, hotels, shops, etc. It's located in a small canyon-type area, hence the name "Glitter Gulch". Glitter Gulch is where most of the hotels and gift shops are. What it offers is convenience. The winter season often times won't have even one business open for business. The population in the winter drops to three or less people.

Alaska

There are many other ghost towns in Alaska and other places that are relics of mining camps here. These are just a few of the most popular.

Beautiful Scenic Drives to Take

Road trips are one of my favorite activities. Whether they are short, several hour excursions, or several days of driving to a specific destination, they can be amazingly fun times. It wasn't that long ago that 'Sunday drives' were a common family tradition. Great music, friends and family always add to the experience of a road trip, even if you have no set destination point.

Every drive is a scenic drive in Alaska. Just driving out of Anchorage (either way – North or South) is an opportunity to see beautiful landscapes and wildlife. The 14 mile drive from the Parks Highway to the little town of Talkeetna offers spectacular views of the Alaska Range. Here are a few more scenic drives to explore.

The Denali Park Road – This 90 mile road into Denali National Park and Preserve (from the visitor's center to Kantishna) has it all – awesome views and if you keep your eyes peeled, numerous wildlife. On this road I have seen dall sheep, wolves, wolverines, bear, golden eagles and more. You can only drive this road once a year when the road lottery is held and you can win the chance to drive it yourself. Otherwise, take the bus and enjoy the ride.

Hatcher Pass Scenic Drive – To drive north from Anchorage isn't as immediately stunning as if you were to drive south, but both routes provide amazing scenery to behold. A favorite of artists and photographers alike.

Glenn Highway goes north east to Palmer, and if you continue you can take a mountain roadway to beautiful Hatcher Pass for the incredible beauty it offers.

Matanuska Glacier off Glenn Highway

Matanuska Glacier Scenic Drive – To take this drive the Glenn Highway to Palmer. You'll find going east that it turns and twists along the Matanuska river, a valley region between beautiful interior and coastal mountains.

Turnagain Arm

Turnagain Arm Drive – the Seward Highway, south of Anchorage takes you along the shores of Turnagain Arm, some say the most beautiful highways in America. Definitely one to explore!

Eklutna Lake Scenic Drive – This scenic drive is 22 miles and brings you to Chugach State Park. It is curvy and runs alongside the Eklutna River and the glacier Eklutna Lake.

Alaska

Old Glenn Highway Scenic Drive – A back road interesting to travel, is a 19 mile country road known as Old Glenn Highway to Palmer. It runs through the middle of Alaska's farm lands and is quiet and beautiful. This road goes to recreation and state parks that offer hiking trails, petting zoos and beautiful terrain to discover in the regions under Pioneer Peak and Chugach Mountains.

Nash Road – One obscure road trip is driving down Nash Road. A few miles into the drive, there's a marked entrance to part of the Iditarod Trail, making it a great place for hiking in the summer, or cross country skiing in winter months.

Seward Highway

Anchorage to Seward (The Seward Highway) – This stunning drive starts with 2 hours of beauty along the intense coastal area of Turnagain Arm, and the majestic Chugach Mountain areas. Bring your camera!

Portage Valley and Whittier Tunnel Drive – Do a road trip through Portage Valley to visit Portage Glacier, worth your time! You may want to make it a longer trip and keep going to Whittier to see the marine region of Prince William Sound.

Skilak Lake Road – This drive would be an eighteen mile, circular gravel road and is amazing for seeing wildlife, lakes and glaciers on the Kenai Peninsula.

Arctic Valley Road Scenic Drive – From Anchorage, drive north to mile 6.1 on the Glenn Highway, then head up Arctic Valley road which is winding and steep. It's only a 45 minute drive, but offers beautiful scenery and amazing views of Cook Inlet, Anchorage and if it's a clear day, Denali.

Parks Highway – This drive is 323 miles long and connects Fairbanks to Anchorage. It crosses some of the most beautiful regions such as Denali Park and Mt. McKinley.

Pasagshak Bay Road – This is a 17 mile stretch of road in which Alaska Aerospace Corporation launch site is found at the end. The road offers access to popular fishing spots, state parks, rivers and places for surf sports.

Anton Larsen Bay Road – Drive southwest from Nome, the road then curves northward. On this short scenic drive you'll discover salmon streams, habitat for various wildlife and good options for recreation activities in the winter. There is a Coast Guard golf course, and a beautiful bay that's protected, good for both beachcombing, and sea kayaking.

Chiniak Highway – You'll find this scenic drive curvy and follows the coast line from Kodiak, its a forty two mile highway. Along the route you'll see the U.S. Coast Guard Station, long ocean inlets, salmon streams and beautiful beaches.

Monashka Bay Road – This road is only 12 miles long and is the shortest out of Kodiak. On this path you'll see beautiful landscapes of tide pools, coastal area, hiking trails, a museum and a white sandy beach. Rezanof Drive becomes Monashka Bay Road.

Nome-Taylor Highway Scenic Drive – This is called several names, Beam Road, Kougarok Road or Nome-Taylor Road, takes 2 hours and is 85 miles long. This is a great historic drive to visit the gold rush era as it goes past many old mining claims in the region.

Nome-Council Highway Scenic Drive – This route is 72 miles in length and takes 2 hours. This is the road to get to the town of Council. When you go east out of town, you'll discover grasslands, coastal flats and sandy beaches along the shores of the Bering Sea, for roughly 30 miles before you start turning inland again.

Nome-Teller Highway Scenic Drive – This route is 73 miles west and takes about 2 hours. The population in Teller is less than 300 people, 85% of which are Eskimo. It was once a boomtown in the gold rush that once had a population of 5,000 people.

The Glacier Highway – The Glacier Highway may not be entirely in Alaska, but it's the closest point in Alaska that you can drive to. It has it all – glaciers, bears, the little town of Hyder and the Fish Creek Wildlife Observation Site.

Alaska

The Alaska Highway

The Alaska Highway – A famous route that still attracts travelers, it goes from Dawson Creek, B.C. to Delta Junction Alaska. It's a total of 1,390 miles long, and with the fairly recently straightened road in many areas, is a wonder to explore.

The Richardson Highway – This drive provides good views of the Alaska pipeline and takes you to Valdez, a port city of Alaska.

The Denali Highway – The Denali Highway stretches 135 miles between the Richardson and the Parks Highway. The road isn't paved but well worth the drive.

The Alaska Railroad

Alaska

The Alaska Railroad – Ok, so this isn't a car drive, but it's a great trip and a great way to see Alaska without having to do any of the work. The railroad covers more than 500 miles and visits some great destinations. The train goes between Anchorage and Fairbanks, along with Whittier, Seward and Girdwood. There is flagstop service along the way. If you ride the train to Hurricane, you'll cross over the enormous Hurricane Gulch. The bridge is a huge 296 feet above the water below. It's an historic adventure to ride one of the last flag stop trains in America, that has been transporting people to remote areas since 1923. You can get off the train anywhere you want on this 55 mile ride. Some folks opt to fish, hike or are seeking a remote cabin to visit. When you are ready to return, you simply wave a flag for the train to stop for you.

Special Attractions and Must-See Places to Visit

There are many treasures in Alaska, including some must see places to experience. Some are more obscure than others. Here, in no particular order, are some that I've discovered.

Manley Hot Springs Greenhouses and Dart Farms, drive Elliot Highway north, and west of Fairbanks for a road trip through the stunning mountains and valleys. The tiny town of Manley Hot Springs is at the end of the Elliot, 152 miles from Fox. About 100 people live there along with a handful of dog teams. It is best known for its privately owned and managed hot springs pools. Hot springs bubble up to a greenhouse fed by the springs. There are 3 concrete baths where soaking can be done. While soaking in the baths, one can see in the greenhouse luscious vegetables, fruits and flowers. For $5,00 a person per hour, the greenhouse may be rented as your private spa.

Also recommended is flightseeing tours, especially if you want to see Mt. McKinley from a bird's eye view or land on a glacier. Many of them fly out of Talkeetna but I'm sure they're available in other areas of Alaska too.

The historic town of Talkeetna is located at the foot of Mt. McKinley (Denali). It displays a stunning panoramic sighting of the Alaska Range that is popular for photographers, artists, and others who enjoy nature and beautiful scenery. There are many things to do in Talkeetna from fishing, boat tours, sightseeing, float trips, hiking, mushing, skiing, mountain climbing, and shopping. The mayor is a cat named Stubbs.

Alaska

Northern Lights Aurora Borealis

Chena Hot Springs Resort was discovered about a century ago. Currently it is the most developed hot spring in Alaska. What makes it famous is it's healing mineral water, while viewing the incredible Aurora Borealis in the winter. The Aurora Ice Museum is also a great place to visit as well with stunning ice sculptures and other ice art.

Ketchikan

Bering Sea Crab Boat Tours in Ketchikan. This tour gives visitors the opportunity to watch crab, shrimp, salmon and other sealife hauled up on deck.

Yet another Talkeetna treasure is the Walter Harper (he was the first person to reach the summit of Mt. McKinley) Ranger Station. This is where people can stop to get permits for Mt. Foraker and Mt. McKinley and orientation of the mountains. Park & climbing information for the Alaska Range, a bookstore and summer interpretive programs can be found at the center.

Mount McKinley Climbers Memorial. This memorial is dedicated to the bravery and stories of those who risked their lives to explore some of Alaska's tallest mountains. Found here are granite plaques and gardens in Talkeetna's downtown. Airplane propellers can be found on the graves of bush pilots who have died.

The Glacier Bay National Park cruise from Juneau is a popular attraction among visitors as well.

Gastineau Channel

In Juneau, try the Mt. Roberts Tram Ride. This very exhilarating tour departs from the cruise dock right in Juneau. Ascend more than 2,000 feet in the tram for a panoramic view of Gastineau Channel and the surrounding mountains in the area. This is an unforgettable experience.

Alaska

Zip line tours are a blast! Custom zip cables and platforms allow people the excitement of zipping through tree tops at high speeds. These may range anywhere from 70' - 2,500' or more! There are some located in Talkeetna, Juneau and Skagway, although there may be more that I'm not aware of.

Kodiak Bear

Kodiak, also known as the Emerald Isle, is probably the most famous of all of the Alaska islands. The Kodiak Archipelago is comprised of roughly 5,000 square miles. It is a wilderness consisting of rivers, mountains, glacier carved valleys, coastlines and islands. The Kodiak brown bear is comparable in size to the polar bear.

Deep sea charter fishing for salmon and halibut. Kodiak, Sitka, Seward, Homer – Take your pick but bring back the catch!

Glacier/Wildlife cruise into Kenai Fjords National Park is an amazing adventure to take in.

River rafting. You might opt for a scenic float trip or whitewater adventure, but whichever you choose, it'll be a time to remember. These are a great way to really enjoy nature in Alaska. Prime areas for rafting include: near Denali on the Nenana River, Talkeetna on the Talkeetna, Susitna and Chulitna Rivers, the Kenai Peninsula on the Kenai or Sixmile Rivers, the Matanuska River about two hours north of Anchorage or the Inside Passage, Mendenhall River or other locations.

Visit Kennicott mining district inside Wrangell-St. Elias National Park. It's interesting to view the copper mine's ruins, which were the most money producing mine in the state. You might even find a piece of malachite or turquoise in the area. The small town next door of McCarthy, shows a bit of the way Alaska was in years past. Kennicott was declared a National Historic Landmark in 1986. Activities that can be done on your visit to Kennecott are ice climbing, glacier hiking and exploring the mill that was abandoned.

McCarthy is a census designated location in the Valdez-Cordova area. The population was 28 at the 2010 census.

McCarthy grew as a place that provided illicit services, in part because in nearby Kennicott prostitution and alcohol were banned. It rapidly grew into a town complete with a school, gym, a hospital, brothel and a bar. The Northwestern and Copper River Railway arrived in McCarthy in 1911. By 1938, most of the copper was gone and the town had pretty much been abandoned and the railroad quit services as well. Over $200 million worth of ore was mined from the area over 30 years, making it one of the most prolific concentrations of copper worldwide.

McCarthy and Kennecott areas rank as one of America's most endangered landmarks by National Trust for Historic Places.

Another popular hiking location is the abandoned mines of Erie, Jumbo and Bonanza. Each of these are full day, strenuous hikes. Erie mine can be a very intensely frightening hike however, due to traveling along cliffs that overlook Stairway Icefall. It should be done with great care and by experienced hikers only.

Stay at Denali National Park. Take the bus and get off to hike at Toklat or take the bus all the way to Wonder Lake and Kantishna.

Alaska Native Heritage Center is a great place to visit. The museum and cultural center share the traditional heritage and history of Alaska's eleven major cultural peoples. Guests enjoy storytelling through first hand engaging styles, authentic native dances and songs, art demos and much more. Great opportunities for old and young alike abound here.

Seward Exit Glacier, is the only portion of the park that can be accessed by road. Beautiful trails invite one to walk, either on your own, or a ranger-led walk, and you can get close to an active glacier. You can see up close and personal how a glacier can re-structure a landscape and how vegetative life brings new life to previously barren rocky land.

Alaska Sea Life Center - This is a must-visit place while in Alaska, not only is it a public aquarium, but its also a marine mammal rehab, the only permanent one in Alaska. Located at Resurrection Bay in Seward, it is dedicated to both public education and research of northern marine sealife.

While in Fairbanks, another must- see place is the Museum of the North by University of Alaska. Amazing exhibits to be seen of wildlife, Alaska's people, and even contemporary Alaskan Native art all provide a rich tapestry of the history and culture of this state.

Riverboat Discovery III, is a four hour boat ride tour of the Tanana and Chena rivers. It possess glass enclosed heated decks, and open sun decks for viewing. Although with the beautiful area, you get a mini lesson of various history in the area during the narration, which has proven to be engaging and humorous at times. This is a visit back in time with the old fashioned paddle boat.

Goldstream Dredge No. 8 – This is a historic mechanical engineering landmark, and is open to the public for educational and historic preservation purposes. In the summer, tours of gold panning and of the dredge are available for a small price. This was a ladder dredge used from 1928 – 1959 by the Fairbanks Exploration Co. Here's a tutorial on how to pan for gold you might enjoy http://youtu.be/PxfcAhS08u0.

A visit to Beluga Point is worth doing. It's located at Turnagain Arm and is an outpost near the waters, along the Seward Highway south of Anchorage. Often beluga white whales can be seen here.

Valdez – kayaking to Columbia Glacier is a great activity and place to see, as is Homer Alaska.

Fairbanks – hiking to both Granite Tors and China Dome are very popular, as is Williwaw Lakes and Anchorage Wolverine Peak.

Seward – A nine hour cruise through the Kenai Fjords is a high point for many travelers.

Inside Passage cruise from Vancouver to Seward or vice versa is a very popular choice of cruise packages that can be found.

Going to the McHugh Creek picnic area and trailhead (found along Turnagain Arm) is a cool place to visit. From the trails along the inlet sometimes beluga whales can be seen and the bore tides are beautiful.

Another interesting place to take in is the Robert G. White Large Animal Research Station in Fairbanks, at the University of Alaska. Locals call it LARS for short, and is found on a former homestead close to UA's campus. It provides education and research in high latitude biology and maintains colonies of large animals. It also conducts community outreach and educational opportunities for the public.

Chickaloon (Glenn Highway) - a must do 3 hour ice trekking hike at Chickaloon Native Village. Culturally rich, and educational, the Ahtna Athabascan Tribe is located in Sutton, which is off the Glenn Highway about about 1 1/2 hours from Anchorage. The Ahtna Athabascan tribe has inhabited this region for many years. You'll see amazing mountains, glaciers and boreal forests.

Seward and Whittier – day boat cruise for wildlife/glaciers viewing and great for sea kayaking.

Admiralty Island, Tracy Arm /Fords Terror Wilderness, Baranof Warm Springs, Frederick Sound, and Thomas Bay, all offer unique traits of beauty and all are sources of solitude if that's what you are seeking.

Alaska

Don't miss visiting the North Pole where Santa Claus lives while you are in the area! Going to the North Pole any time of year, you'll find festive Christmas decorations, light poles, and holiday street names. Be sure to also cruise down Santa Claus Lane seeing the large candy cane light poles. Of course, you also can't miss stopping at the Santa Claus House, the house Santa himself lives in.

If you love to ski or snowboard, a good place to check out is Aleyska a beautiful ski resort and hotel found at Girdwood, only 40 minutes from Anchorage. The ski resort is famous for its very deep snow pack and steep terrain, giving a real challenge to experienced skiers.

During the summer in Girdwood hikes are popular in the old growth rainforest of Winner Creek Trail.

Alaska Bird and Farm Animal Rescue in Anchorage is a non profit bird & farm animal rescue facility. They administer medical aid to the injured if needed, and use most birds & animals for education. They have gone out to the community schools, hospitals, and military bases for deployment parties, or fund raising events to help the event, and to give children a chance to learn about animals and to pet them.

Go fishing – Alaska is a fisherman's haven with many options to choose from. Rivers host salmon, rainbow trout, and other fish. You will need to prepare by applying for a fishing license before your journey. Some choices could be fishing in an idyllic quiet stream by yourself, or hire a charter for either just a day, or a whole week. Alaska is home to 21 species of recognized sport fish that attracts anglers literally from around the world.

Alaska

Walmikes in Trapper Creek is a unique Alaskan shopping experience with anything and everything. Defies descripti only a definite must see.

Tok is a cool town to check out because it is a border tov the Canadian border. Very popular with dog mushing.

Trace the steps of the Iditarod National Historic Trail – This is a 1000 + mile trail connecting 50 miles north of Seward, via Iditarod, finishing in Nome. Explorers used this trail most commonly by dog sleds to move goods across the landscape, as the Native Alaskans taught them. It's a popular trail for hiking in the summer months, or in winter by dogsled, cross country skiing, snowshoeing, or snowmobile. Beautiful scenic exploration at its finest!

Dalton Highway

The perilous Dalton Highway – is a drive known as Alaska Route 11. The highway is 414 miles long, going north of Fairbanks and concluding near the Arctic Ocean. It was a supply road for supporting the Trans-Alaska Pipeline and one of the most remote highways in America. There are only 3 towns along the route, so be sure you bring plenty of supplies and food.

There is still gold that can be found in Alaska, both in streams and mountains, it just takes some work to discover it. There are several places in the state that can be searched for free. Consider Fairbanks, where it all began, although panning can be experienced just about anywhere, such as the Dalton highway and the beach near Nome.

Alaska

Consider visiting the most northern city in the United States, called Barrow and sometimes known as the 'end of the earth'. It could be called a more obscure destination, especially since it can only be accessed by plane. No roads connect this town to the rest of the state. It has a population of less than 5,000 people. Due to its extreme north location, it is in total darkness between 50 to 70 days each year. Then when the sun does shine, it doesn't set at all, from May to early August. Visiting the Pigniq archaeological site in Barrow is an educational excursion. There are sixteen dwelling mounds originating from a culture that lived from 500-900 AD. It's a great place to watch the Northern Lights during the darkness season.

Anchorage has a museum, located at the Rasmuson Center, that is a must see for visitors. It is one of excellence that strives to exhibit, interpret, and preserve the history & art of the state, and the polar North region.

The Pratt Museum in Homer is an excellent place to see. This historical museum helps to preserve the stories in the Kachemak Bay area and is a popular gathering spot for education and inspiration for people wanting to learn about

Alaska

this region. It does this by exhibits, collections and various programs in art, science and culture. It also has a popular SeeBird camera (Gull Cam) to provide wildlife viewing for visitors.

Annual Festivals and Fairs

Annual festivals and fairs are great family friendly gatherings to take in and enjoy. Below we'll list a few to check out, but it's not a complete, exhaustive list. Where I could, I've provided a link for more complete details and logistics for each festival and fair, as it does vary each year.

Alaska Folk Festival http://www.akfolkfest.org/ early to mid April Juneau, Alaska/ In this festival the community enjoys various performances from professionals, to school groups, with much in-between. It's free of charge to attend this fun event.

Stikine River Migratory Bird and Garnet Festival (http://www.wrangell.com/birdingfestival/stikine-river-birding-festival-april-24-26-2014), 3rd week in April,

Wrangell, Alaska. This festival is held the 3rd week in April and signals the start of spring, celebrating the arrival of the biggest spring gathering of bald eagles in the U.S, sometimes as many as 3,000 eagles. In addition to the eagles there can also be 10,000 Sand Hill cranes, 200,000 various shorebirds and 15,000 snow geese to be seen. The festival also features an arts and craft fair, a public market, golf tournaments, concerts, kayaking workshops and many opportunities for birding.

Gold Rush Days (http://www.traveljuneau.com/events/) mid June Juneau, Alaska. Running for several decades now, the popular Gold Rush days began in Juneau, in 1990 featuring annual logging and mining competitions. Being a 2 day event, the first day focuses on mining events and Sunday concentrates on logging events. This is a great family event as well, and has many activities for children including hand mucking, gold panning and carnival games.

Fairbanks Summer Arts Festival (http://www.fsaf.org/) end July Fairbanks, Alaska. This event takes place on the University of Alaska's campus and draws people worldwide to see over 100 artists in many art mediums, including various performances as well. This is one not to miss!

Golden Days (http://fairbankschamber.org/goldendays/) late July Fairbanks, Alaska. Golden Days is a fun, family friendly festival that celebrates the establishment of Fairbanks, and draws people from all over the world to this event. It lasts 5 days and some highlights are rubber duck races, comedy night, street fair, kids events, historic reenactments and more.

Athabscan Old-Time Fiddlers Festival (https://www.facebook.com/pages/The-Athabascan-Fiddlers-Association/342325469003) early November Fairbanks, Alaska

This is a 4 day festival that is a tribute to music, that changed from when the fiddle was first introduced to the Athabascan Indians by the Arcadian and French fur trappers over a century ago. This event attracts musicians from both Alaska and well into Canada.

Sitka Whalefest (http://www.sitkawhalefest.org/) held in November

This annual event has now been running more than fifteen years, attesting to its popularity. It both educates and entertains visitors to the marine mammals of the region. It also hosts marine mammal and whale watching trips, workshops, and discussions. There is also a concert as well as other community events to participate in.

Alaska Bald Eagle Festival (http://baldeagles.org/festival)mid November Haines Alaska. This festival on the Chilkat River's main highlight is the 3,000 eagles that gather in the area, attracting nature lovers, photographers and visitors from all over. There are events like special guest speakers, photo workshops, the release of rehabilitated bald eagles, guided eagle viewing to name a few. Such an amazing experience to have.

Girdwood Forest Fair (http://www.girdwoodforestfair.com) – July –
This is a family event with a forest fair parade, hand crafted items made by local artists, entertainers and amazing foods to experience. Check it out.

Deltana Fair (http://deltanafair.com) – Delta Junction – July August – fair and music festival.

Tanana Valley State Fair (http://www.tananavalleystatefair.com) – Fairbanks – August

Kenai Peninsula State Fair (http://www.kenaipeninsulafair.com) – Ninilchik, in August. This state fair is both educational, entertaining and a fun way for families and the community to connect. There's also an art & fiber festival not to be missed.

Alaska State Fair (http://www.alaskastatefair.org/site) – Palmer – August/September

Kodiak Rodeo and State Fair (http://74-220-216-33.bluehost.com/currents/previous-issues/13-august-2010/96-

kodiak-rodeo-and-state-fair-gear-up-for-the-main-event.html)
– September – Kodiak

Anchorage Folk Festival (http://www.anchoragefolkfestival.org) – Anchorage – April – celebrating live community folk music, dance and fun.

Great Alaska Beer and Barley Wine Festival (http://auroraproductions.net/docs/2014 BBW Application.pdf) – Anchorage – January – over 200 beers and barley wines from over 50 regional brewers featured.

Bard-A-Thon (http://www.fstalaska.org/bard-a-thon) – Fairbanks – April – The yearly reading the entire collection of Shakespeare's work is read by the community 24 hours a day until completed.

Iron Dog (http://www.irondog.org) – January – Wasilla – Nome - Fairbanks. This is the world's longest snowmobile race, now over 2,000 miles. It starts in Big Lake, goes to Nome, then finishes in Fairbanks. Survival skills are critical due to going through some of the most rugged, grueling and remote terrain, on top of harsh winter conditions. It is know to be the toughest snowmobile race ever. Each team consists of 2 people and 2 snowmobiles.

Kachemak Bay Shorebird Festival (http://www.homeralaska.org/visit-homer/events-homer/kachemak-bay-shorebird-festival) – May in Homer Naturalists, guides and expert speakers will impart their wisdom of birding as they lead though workshops, presentations, field events and even bus, boat and kayak tours. This is Alaska's largest wildlife festival and participants have over 50 options of events to choose from. It caters to both beginning level bird watching, to advanced ornithology workshops. Children's activities are also offered.

Annual Eagle River-Chugiak Bear Paw Festival Vendor Court (http://www.bearpawfestival.org) – Anchorage – July. There is live entertainment, shopping and great food to be found at the annual Bear Paw Festival. There are also carnival rides and games that everyone is sure to enjoy!

Mayor's Marathon (http://www.goseawolves.com/SportSelect.dbml?DB_OEM_ID=13400&SPID=145508&SPSID=865211) the Summer Solstice in June, Anchorage. This yearly marathon is run with the scenic beauty of the Alaskan wilderness. Its a 26.2 mile race, or there is a half marathon, a 4 mile race or a 1.6 mile youth race and even a marathon relay race, that can be participated in, with people choosing which one they want to do.

Seward Silver Salmon Derby (http://www.seward.com/welcome-to-seward-alaska/signature-events/seward-silver-salmon-derby-august). This derby is one of the largest and oldest in Alaska. It's very popular with both residents and visiting anglers from around the world. Anglers compete for the biggest Coho salmon, and also to catch specially tagged fish for various prizes and bragging rights.

Fur Rendezvous Festival (http://www.alaska.org/detail/fur-rondezvous-festival). The 'Fur Rondy' celebrates the enjoyment of Alaskan winters. Bundle up to keep warm, and check out the native arts market, outhouse races, snow sculpture contest, snowshoe softball, and other super fun events in late February.

Mount Marathan Race (http://www.adn.com/mount-marathon-race) began officially as an organized run in 1915 and has become a favored tradition of Independence Day activities in Seward. They even hold a mini-marathon for youngsters.

Midnight Sun Festival Fairbanks (http://downtownfairbanks.com/events/midnight-sun-festival) A family friendly 12 hour street fair with awesome food booths, crafts, live music and many other activities, not to be missed.

Alyeska Slush Cup (http://www.alaska.org/detail/alyeska-slush-cup)Third weekend of April. This competition is a combination of skiing and strange costumes as they attempt to skid across a long stretch of freezing water on skis. Super fun!

Alyeska Resort Blueberry Festival (http://www.alaska.org/detail/alyeska-resort-blueberry-festival) August. Alaskan blueberries are so delicious and popular, that Girdwood annually hosts a celebration of blueberry season. This is a family friendly gathering and is a great reason to visit the gorgeous area.

Seward 4th of July Celebration (http://www.alaska.org/detail/seward-4th-of-july-celebration)

Seward Halibut Tournament (http://www.alaska.org/detail/seward-halibut-tournament). Sometimes visitors tend to think of Seward in connection with Silver Salmon, but halibut are also amazing in this region. The halibut tournament draws fisherman and anglers from all over Alaska to participate in this event.

Copper River Wild Salmon Festival (http://www.alaska.org/detail/copper-river-wild-salmon-festival) The last weekend in July, this popular fishing village sponsors an amazing salmon festival in Cordova. Some events that happen are fun runs, a salmon BBQ, live music, seafood cook-offs and youth education programs.

Blueberry Arts Festival (http://www.alaska.org/detail/blueberry-arts-festival) August in Ketchikan.

Talkeetna Trio (http://www.alaska.org/detail/talkeetna-trio) Early February

The Talkeetna Trio is a race using fat bikes only.

Burning Basket (http://homernews.com/homer-features/backyard/2013-09-18/10th-annual-burning-basket-%E2%80%98enjoy%E2%80%99) Homer – Every September

The Great Alaska Aviation Gathering (http://www.greatalaskaaviationgathering.org/)

Willow Winter Carnival (http://waco-ak.org/carnival.php) This yearly winter carnival has been going more than fifty years. It's held the last weekend in January and beginning of February. It offers the largest winter fireworks show, large Bingo cash pots, foot races, fat tire bike races, dog sled races and more. Its a large attraction for residents and tourists alike.

Alaska

Iditarod Sled Dog Race (Ceremonial Start) (http://www.alaska.org/detail/iditarod-sled-dog-race-ceremonial-start)

This is the renowned sled dog race that starts in Anchorage downtown area, the 1st Saturday of March. The first leg of this race is held on city streets lined with fans cheering. The next six miles goes south and east through Anchorage's greenbelts, parks and trail systems.

World Eskimo-Indian Olympics (http://www.alaska.org/detail/world-eskimo-indian-olympics) Fairbanks

Sitka Seafood Festival (http://www.alaska.org/detail/sitka-seafood-festival)

This celebration is an incredible festival for foodies, offering on opening night, a full 5 course seafood dinner, deliciously prepared by chefs. This is a chance to sample all the amazing seafood found in the area.

Iditarod Sled Dog Race Restart (http://www.alaska.org/detail/iditarod-sled-dog-race-restart)
"The Last Great Race" begins in Willow, the first Sunday of March at 2:00 PM. Mushers exit the gate every 2 minutes, while thousands of fans cheer on the dog sled teams. This is a classic Alaskan experience, and one that shouldn't be missed!

Kodiak Crab Festival (http://www.alaska.org/detail/kodiak-crab-festival)
This 5 day festival has many traditional and unique competitions, including a survival suit race.

Alaska

Homer Highland Games

(http://www.alaska.org/detail/homer-highland-games)

Susitna 100 Miles & Little Su

50K (http://www.alaska.org/detail/susitna-100-miles-little-su-50k) Mid February

Iditarod Restart Golf Tournament

(http://www.alaska.org/detail/iditarod-restart-golf-tournament). Seven days after Willow sponsors the Iditarod Sled Dog Restart, a golf tournament is held on the groomed trail from the dog sled race. This unique tournament attracts 100 cold weather golfers for a 9 hole tourney. It is said that when the golf balls bounce on groomed snow, it has a similar feel to real grass. There is a two club limit per person.

Palmer Colony Days (http://www.alaska.org/detail/palmer-colony-days) June

Homer Yacht Club (http://www.alaska.org/detail/homer-yacht-club)

Southeast Alaska State Fair (http://www.alaska.org/detail/southeast-alaska-state-fair)

Homer Jackpot Halibut Derby (http://www.alaska.org/detail/homer-jackpot-halibut-derby). This is the longest running derby in the state, its proud of offering the largest prizes for catching halibut.

Luminary Ski (http://www.alaska.org/detail/luminary-ski) Divide Ski Trails at Mile 12 of the Seward Highway on New Year's Eve.

Alaska

Talkeetna Bluegrass Festival

(http://www.alaska.org/detail/talkeetna-bluegrass-festival)

Wearable Arts (http://www.alaska.org/detail/wearable-arts)

Seward Music and Arts Festival

(http://www.alaska.org/detail/seward-music-and-arts-festival)

Seward Holiday Arts and Craft Fair

(http://www.alaska.org/detail/seward-holiday-arts-and-craft-fair)

Colony Christmas Celebration

(http://www.palmerchamber.org/events/colony-christmas.html). The town of Palmer hosts a 3 day holiday celebration the second weekend in December. There is a parade of lights, fireworks, reindeer and horse sleigh rides and a gorgeous tree lighting ceremony.

Sitka Jazz Festival (http://www.alaska.org/detail/sitka-jazz-festival)

Barrow Whaling Festival (http://www.alaska.org/detail/barrow-whaling-festival)

Iditarod Trail Invitational (http://www.alaska.org/detail/iditarod-trail-invitational) Late February. This one is a bike, run or cross country ski race for people.

Talkeetna Winterfest (http://www.alaska.org/detail/talkeetna-winterfest)

Talkeenta sponsors an annual event in December known as the Talkeetna Winterfest. It holds a very popular Bachelor Society Ball & Auction, where bidding sometimes commands as much as $1K for a drink and dance at the ball. It is held the first Saturday of December.

Kachemak Bay Wooden Boat Festival (http://www.alaska.org/detail/kachemak-bay-wooden-boat-festival)

Held annually in September, the Bachemak Bay wooden boat society sponsors this very fun festival. It includes a tour of the waters, including a World War II era wood tug boat, that has been altered for charter usage, knot tying and other marine demonstrations, kids' boat building, bronze casting, and net mending. Great local entertainment as well that's not to be missed.

White Mountains 100 (http://www.alaska.org/detail/white-mountains-100) Late March. A 100 mile human powered adventure in remote and beautiful interior Alaska, near Fairbanks.

Alaska Day Festival (http://www.alaska.org/detail/alaska-day-festival)

This festival celebrates when Alaska was purchased by the United States from Russia. It has an educational element to it with historical reenactments and panel discussions. There's a parade led by Seattle's Fire Department pipe and drum regiment, a gala ball and other family friendly events.

Copper River Shorebird Festival (http://www.alaska.org/detail/copper-river-shorebird-festival). This is an incredible gathering of literally hundred of thousands of shorebirds at The Delta. Geese, ducks, swans, and bald eagles are some of the species found here.

Valdez May Day Fly-in & Air Show (http://www.valdezalaska.org/events/valdez-fly-in-and-air-show)

The Seldovia Summer Solstice Music Festival (http://seldoviamusicfestival.wordpress.com/)

The Downtown Solstice Festival (http://www.anchoragedowntown.org/upcoming-events/downtown-summer-solstice-festival/) takes place in Anchorage. There are many fun activities to participate in, if one desires to. The Hero Games is a competition of Alaskan first responders giving it all in obstacle courses, relays and bucket brigades. There are puppet shows for the kids, a huge sandbox, kayak pool. There are some very cool teen pro skateboarders demos, who will demonstrate their amazing skills at the professional level.

Salmonstock (http://www.salmonstock.org/) Ninilchik August

Alaska Hummingbird Festival (http://www.recreation.gov/marketing.do?goto=acm/Explore_And_More/exploreArticles/Spotlight__Alaska_Hummingbird_Festival_in_Ketchikan__Alaska.htm) - Ketchikan, Alaska. The month of April celebrates in Ketchikan the return of migratory birds, but especially the Rufous hummingbird. Event includes art shows, guided hikes, birding opportunities and activities for kids.

Annual Cabin Fever Reliever Day

(http://www.trappercreek.org/events.htm)

2nd weekend in March, Trapper

Annual Fireweed Festival

(http://trappercreekorg.blogspot.com/2013/07/8th-annual-trapper-creek-fireweed.html) The last weekend of July, Trapper Creek residents host a day of great fun, with upscale craft booths, amazing foods to try and live music. There is also a cozy bonfire towards the end of the evening to top off this event.

Kid and Family Friendly Places

There aren't any amusement parks in Alaska, but there are many places that are kid and family friendly to check out. Many of the must see attractions; parks, glaciers and cruises are fun for all ages.

H2Oasis Indoor Waterpark (http://www.h2oasiswaterpark.com) is a 56,000 square foot indoor water park located in Anchorage. H2Oasis offers a wide range of amenities and fun rides: slides, wavepools, even a simulated river that circles the park. H2Oasis also offers water therapy, exercise and swim lessons.

The Alaska Zoo (http://alaskazoo.org/) located in Anchorage. This zoo is a non-profit and serves conservation efforts of sub-Arctic and Arctic climate species as well as helping injured and orphaned animals.

Fairbanks has an amazing 4 hour tour ride on the Riverboat Discovery III (http://riverboatdiscovery.com/), it has both heated glass enclosed decks and open sun decks to cater to people wanting either, depending on the weather. It not only tours the Tanana and Chena Rivers, it also provides an educational opportunity on the culture, geology, history and more of the region. A fun visit honoring times past in a river paddle steam boat.

Visit any one of Alaska's national parks and historic sites for a family fun day.

The Great Alaskan Lumberjack Show (http://alaskanlumberjackshow.com) in Ketchikan is the beginning of this community's walking tour. It is located on the banks of a salmon stream loaded with fish jumping, that are going up Ketchikan Creek. Lumberjacks battle each other in competitions in sawing, tree climbing, chopping, and axe throwing. There is much history to take in on this event.

Pioneer Park in Fairbanks (http://www.co.fairbanks.ak.us/pioneerpark) brings you back in time to the gold rush days. There is a Native Alaskan village, a riverboat, golf, railroad and much more to take in.

Denali National Park and Preserve Dog Sled Demonstration
Denali National Park (http://www.nps.gov/dena/planyourvisit/sled-dog-demonstrations.htm) is an amazing place to visit for any age. Dogs & rangers working together demonstrate the traditional mode of travel for Alaska. It provides half hour programs to

tour the kennels and visit Denali's Alaskan huskies, and is open to guests all year around. They help to provide historic preservation and education of both the pioneer and Native Alaskan's experiences in the region. These are the only sled dogs that assist in helping protect a national park, wilderness and wildlife. Denali's is a working kennel in which the huskies are used every winter to patrol the park where motorized vehicles are not permitted.

In fact, there are many tours you can take with dog sled rides. There are generally two different kinds of tours – Party on wheels. You'll visit a kennel and be surrounded by the cacophony (and smell) of dogs, meet team members and cuddle some of the puppies. You typically get to ride on one of the wheeled carts (on the ground, not snow) that the dogs use for training or flying to, and riding on the snow. You'll combine about 20 minutes of dog sledding on a glacier with either a fixed-wing plane or helicopter flightseeing trip.

Alaska Raptor Center (http://www.alaskaraptor.org) is a rehab center located in Sitka for raptors. It is a large 17 acre establishment on the border of the Tongass forest and Indian River. Its main mission is the care of injured and sick hawks, falcons, eagles, raptors owls and other birds of prey that come in from all over the state. Part of the mission and goals of the center is also for the birds to go back to the wild after they are healed. Many are retrained before this occurs, such as help with flying and other survival skills to ensure their success. Many of the birds that cannot live in the wild anymore are shipped to wildlife centers and zoos across the nation, and some of these birds also live as permanent residents at the center.

Community playgrounds in Soldotna, Homer, Seward, Talkeetna and more are always a safe bet with kids and make a good site for a picnic.

The Live @ 5 Summer Concert Series in Talkeetna's Village Park (http://www.talkeetnachamber.org/schedule/event/live-5-summer-concert-series-in-the-village-park) is a family friendly event taking place every Friday night in the summer season in Talkeetna. Live @ 5! was created a few years ago by the combined efforts of the Talkeetna Chamber of Commerce and the Denali Arts Council as a way to showcase the great musicians of the area, as well as provide family and community friendly activities to add to the health of the town's park.

Alaska Wildlife Conservation Center (http://www.alaskawildlife.org) exists for the purposes of conservation efforts of wildlife, animal care, and education. They take in injured and orphaned animals when they are unable to care for themselves in the wild, to the Wood Bison Restoration Project.

White Pass Railway in Skagway (http://www.wpyr.com) During the Klondike Gold rush, in 1898 a narrow gauge railroad was built. This railway was considered to be impossible to build. However, after only 26 months, it was completed.

Creamer's Field Migratory Waterfowl Refuge (http://www.creamersfield.org/Visit_Us.html) located in Fairbanks. The refuge consists of 2,000 acres of woods, fields and wetlands. Barns, a farmhouse and twelve acres are listed with the National Register of Historic Places, and is wonderful to visit.

Islands and Ocean Visitor Center (http://www.islandsandocean.org) in Homer is a wonderful place to visit. An indoor displays re-creations of Aleutian artifacts and a camp where you can see the work of biologists Many of the programs are outdoor experiences, like walking the beach and watching for abundant wildlife in the area.

Anan Bear and Wildlife Observatory in Wrangell (http://www.wrangell.com/visitorservices/anan-bear-and-wildlife-observatory). Anan Creek is an historic Tlingit native fishing area found on the south end of Wrangell Island. In the summer months there are large runs of salmon to Anan Creek, which draws large numbers of black and brown bears. There's a part covered observatory deck in which people can see the bears clearly, yet still be safe. The Anan estuary is accessible only by plane or boat.

The Sitka Sound Science Center (http://www.sitkascience.org) offers education, research and increases understanding of the ecosystems in the Gulf of Alaska. It has 3 touch tanks, 5 mounted in the wall aquariums, a large eight hundred gallon viewing tank, preserved specimens and whale bones.

Ketchikan, AlaskaThe Southeast Alaska Discovery Center (http://www.experienceketchikan.com/southeast-alaska-discovery-center.html) has world-class exhibits, and is an Alaska Public Lands Information Center providing expert information on most anything. It also has has an incredible bookstore and gift shop.

The Center for Alaskan coastal Studies (http://www.akcoastalstudies.org) in Homer allows you to Explore Kachemak Bay. Each person is given a personal experience among amazing intertidal life on the beaches and beautiful flowers and trees in the coastal forest.

The University of Alaska Museum of the North (http://www.uaf.edu/museum) located in Fairbanks is a must-visit site, being the only research and teaching museum in the state. There are 1.4 million specimens and artifacts, broken into 10 disciplines, representative of cultural traditions of the Northern region.

Fairbanks Children's Museum in Fairbanks (http://www.fairbankschildrensmuseum.com) Alaska is a great place to take kids for a fun, yet educational excursion.

A Local's Favorite Places

My favorite places to hang out include Talkeetna, a trip on the Hurricane Turn train, McCarthy (mentioned earlier) and Denali. In Talkeetna my favorite places include the Roadhouse, and the Fairview Inn.

The Talkeetna Roadhouse dates back from the early 20th century and is a historically significant Alaskan frontier roadhouse. It served as resting places for miners, prospectors, fur trappers and other visitors who were journeying their way through the territory in the 19th and 20th centuries. The Talkeetna Roadhouse provides meals, showers, laundry and lodging. Known for their delicious desserts and big, hearty breakfasts, the roadhouse is a glimpse into the past.

Also the historic Fairview Inn. The inn accommodated travelers enroute on the Alaska Railroad by opening in 1923. Currently the hotel consists of 6 remodeled rooms, and a bar with live music that features many genres of music, from folk to jazz, rock-n-roll and everything in between. The walls house many vintage photos and memorabilia to take a stroll down memory lane, or discover vintage items, popular in their former glory.

And finally in Talkeetna, my other favorite places include the Overlook, with a beautiful panoramic view of the Alaska Range; the many trails, and the river, (Talkeetna means "the place where the rivers meet"). Talkeetna is situated on the confluence of the Talkeetna, Susitna and Chulitna Rivers.

Another recommendation is the Tsunami Warning Center in Palmer. The West Coast and Alaska Tsunami Warning Center is one of two U.S. Tsunami Warning Centers. The West Coast and Alaska Tsunami Warning Center monitors earthquakes globally and issues warnings for the North American continent should a tsunami be generated that could threaten life and property.

In Denali one of my favorite places is Toklat. The river Toklat is a stunning landscape of massive cliffs and glacial rivers. Dall sheep are quite often viewed on the steep terrain, and sometimes grizzlies are seen in the area's gentler hillsides and riverbeds. Wolves are also often spotted in the region.

Kantishna is another small community in Denali to visit. It was originally a gold mining camp established in 1905. It is located at the junction of Moose Creek and Eureka Creek, three miles to the northwest of Wonder Lake.

Winter sports are always popular here, snowmobiling, skiing, cross country skiing, snowshoeing, and of course, dog sledding.

Dangers & Safety Precautions for Alaska

Alaska is the 8th most dangerous state. The biggest risk in Alaska is the state itself. The terrain here is awesome and treacherous. The environment can kill very easily. Visitors are advised to wear layers as the weather can change dramatically in a short amount of time. Of course, the unforeseen can happen too – like your vehicle breaking down (not uncommon) and then you are stuck. Here's a story about the dangers of Alaska in your very own back yard.

I decided to create a snowshoe trail in my back yard one February. I hadn't broken trail before and it was tough going. About half way through my little trail I fell down and had to take my snowshoes off to get up. There I was, stranded, not 300 feet from my cabin, in thigh deep snow. It took me three hours to get back to the house.

Bears are also a big thing to consider, especially in summer and late fall when they are feeding themselves to prepare for hibernation. When encountering a bear it is best to freeze, because prey runs (a whole new meaning to fast food). Make yourself appear as big as possible. Most seasoned Alaskans hike with a gun to frighten off bears. Pepper spray is good but you got to get close enough to the bear to use it, and not many people have that presence of mind. Shouting helps too. Here's an experience from my own life about an Alaskan bear.

It was September, and the landlord called to tell us about a black bear prowling around the cabin. He had a shed with two freezers full of food so he put up a piece of plywood to cover the door of the shed. The bear left, but came back a few hours later. The plywood didn't bother him. The bear went around to the side and ate through the half log walls of the shed. The bear was maybe ten yards from the cabin. It was like watching the Discovery Channel, only in real life. My housemate had the bear in his gun's aim, but with no bear tags and a mess to clean up afterwards, decided not to shoot. We called the landlord instead. When he came out the bear was quiet and he didn't believe that the bear was in the shed, till he heard the huffing. We decided to call the state troopers. "Sorry about your luck," they said. "Let us know how it turns out".

After shouting a bit, which didn't move the bear (who was comfortable for the winter-- a nice dark place with a food supply), the landlord shot through the shed which did finally send the bear running. Looking at the freezers the next day was amazing. First of all the bear ate 20 salmon and was working on the cheese. It looked like the whole freezer was demolished with one swipe of the bear's paw, which was a stunning sight.

Much of what works with a bear works with a wolf. Remember, don't run. Food runs.

Moose are also dangerous because they can stomp with those long legs. More people have been killed by moose than by bears. Please don't stop and take close up photos of the wildlife. These animals are not tame.

The mudflats are dangerous as well. Mudflats are formed as mud and silt and brought in from various water sources. That is then deposited in lagoons, bays and inlets as tides come in. This all mixes together and creates a muddy quicksand that can be very difficult to get out of. In July of 1988, a very tragic event on the mudflats near Portage, known as

Alaska

Turnagain Arm claimed the life of a young woman. Her left leg sunk to her knee in the silt, and she was unable to get free. Help was summoned, but came too late. The rapid tide coming in was too much and too fast. Hypothermia was also a factor in her death.

Do not go onto the mudflats of Turnagain Arm or Knik Arm ever! While some areas may be drier, thus more sturdy, you might need to cover areas that are wet and more dangerous, visually you might not be able to see much difference between the two conditions. Tides also come in at over ten miles per hour, which causes even more danger to the area. Nothing is worth the risk!

Hypothermia, or cooling of the body's temperature, may occur year around with deadly results. It occurs most commonly when temps are in between 30 - 50 degrees F.

Wet clothes and windy conditions can greatly contribute to the condition, even in the summer, and sometimes a person might even be aware of how cold they are truly getting. When the body gets too cold, it can start to shut down, the brain loses some reasoning capacity, which can lead to distorted thinking and poor judgment. Victims of hypothermia many times can't help themselves, so it's important for people to be aware of this and watch out for each other.

Alaska has 17 percent of the world's earthquakes. In line with that, tsunamis are a big issue too. The most powerful earthquake was the 1964 Good Friday Quake with a magnitude of 9.2 – the most powerful earthquake in North America ever recorded. It lasted four minutes and 38 seconds and caused about 139 deaths. It caused aftershocks for 3 weeks numbering in the thousands.

Fire is another issue in Alaska. Alaska might get wildfires as early as March and as late as December. Alaska Interagency Coordination Center states that an average of 1.7 million acres are burned statewide each year.

Firearms are an important part of the Alaskan culture. Of course, treating them with respect goes without saying, and taking proper safety precautions is critical for the safety of everyone.

In rural communities, it can be quite a while before an ambulance can arrive to help you in an emergency. I know of a woman who died of a heart attack, because it took an hour for the ambulance to arrive at her rural home.

Flooding also is a concern. With all of Alaska's rivers and lakes, being fed by glaciers, snow melt, and rain, flooding becomes a real factor as one of Alaska's dangers.

Highway construction that may have closures, or long delays can also pose safety risk factors to drivers. Almost all construction is during the summer months, when tourist traffic is also at its peak and the highways are busiest. Most roads and highways, even the main ones, are mostly two lane roads. Traffic can really back up for long wait periods, which can lead to some very impatient drivers who may pass other motorists at very dangerous points, to try to make up for lost time.

There are at least 25 different species of mosquitoes found in Alaska. There may be as many as 40 species. They are obnoxious in the summer, along with the whitesocks and the no-see-ums. Bring plenty of insect repellant.

And lastly, one of the most dangerous things in Alaska are unprepared humans. Stock up on any supplies you might even possibly need for the season. Have extra food, water, candles, blankets, and dry clothing easily accessible in case it's needed. Make sure your car is in good working order, good batteries, jumper cables & plenty of gas in the tank at all times. Have a safety kit on hand. Use common sense and don't take unnecessary risks. Alaska is a wilderness and should be respected as such.

Special Seasonal Activities

Alaskans are busy year round. Winter and summer are the two seasons that most special events are held.

The northern lights in the winter are famous. The Aurora Borealis are, natural displays of color that light up the sky as they dance and flicker in many designs and color variations. Seeing them can be unpredictable. They are most clearly seen in March and September. The prime times to see the northern lights is January and February on a clear, cold night. They are best seen from places far removed from city lights. An hour and a half after sunset is usually the best time to see them.

The Midnight Sun Game is held at Growden Memorial Park in Fairbanks. It's a unique baseball game played every summer solstice, and begins at about 10:30 PM, wrapping up around 1:30 AM. Not many baseball games can be played outdoors at that time!

Yukon Quest is a one thousand mile dog sled race in early February. It goes from Fairbanks to Whitehorse, Yukon. The terrain is very rugged with long distances in between checkpoints, giving it the reputation of being the 'toughest race on earth'. The competition consists of fifty dog teams, each having one person as the 'musher' and fourteen dogs per

Alaska

team. The race takes between 10 and 14 days and alternates routes each year. This is a well anticipated event each year, with much preparation going into it.

World Ice Art Championships in late February to the end of March, held in Fairbanks are amazing! The competition and exhibition of the ice art is among the largest in the world for ice sculpting. The finished ice sculptures are lighted the day after the end of the event, and displays works of over one hundred artists from almost 50 different countries. The public is encouraged to watch both the creative process in the beginning stages (the first 2 weeks of March), and to see the completed artwork in the last 2 weeks of March. It is held at the George Horner ice art park in Fairbanks. There are also many other family events and activities one can participate in while there.

The Nenana Ice Classic. Alaska has no state lottery, but this is the closest to it. The point of this 'lottery' is to guess as accurately as possible, the minute the Tanana river breaks up To participate, a person can mail their list of guesses (tickets must be puchased within the state), with $2.50 per guess to the Nenana Ice Classic Office. If you want a copy of your completed entries, also include a SASE.

Complexities of Love, in February at Talkeetna. Singing, dancing, acting and joking are part of this variety show, which is a memorable experience. This a very unique way to experience Valentine's Day.

Public Gardens to Visit

It seems most everyone has a garden in Alaska. With such a unique climate and growing conditions, there are some amazing public gardens, visitors should try to see. Here are a few:

Alaska Botanical Garden Anchorage (http://www.alaskabg.org)– Hardy perennials and native place species are in abundance here. Amazing place to visit!

Glacier Gardens Rainforest (http://www.glaciergardens.com) is located in Juneau and contains over fifty acres of rainforest gardens. These beautiful gardens show upside down flower towers that are truly unique, and a must-see within the Tongass National Forest. The Glacier Rainforest Gardens also shows amazing panoramic views of the Juneau area.

Jewell Gardens in Skagway (http://www.jewellgardens.com) provides a large variety of different types of plants. It also has Alaska's only glassblowing studio open to the public where people can blow their own glass art work. Because of this, there are many glass artworks that can be found around the grounds, made by Garden City glassworks artists.

Mann Leiser Municipal Greenhouse in Anchorage (https://foursquare.com/v/mann-leiser-memorial-greenhouses-anchorage-ak/4e77bf18d1646aa04cee2833) has a tropical greenhouse open for public viewing, with a fish pond and small aviary. The horticulture portion provides thousands of plants to Alaska, and also supplies over 76,000 annual flowers on 81 different sites, among many others. It truly does a very large business that contributes plants, trees, and other related supplies and services to the state.

Alaska

The Jensen-Olson Arboretum (http://www.juneau.org/parkrec/arboretum-main.php) located in Juneau, is a public garden. It contains 800 living plants in its fifteen acres. A beautiful place to behold.

Palmer Municipal Gardens (http://palmergardens.blogspot.com) found on the grounds of the Palmer Museum of History and Art and Visitor Center.

The University of Alaska Fairbanks (http://georgesonbg.org) Georgeson Botanical Garden. Dedicated to plants and conservation of sub-arctic species.

Last Words of Sage Advice From a Local Resident

My first bit of advice would be to wear layers, rather than one big furry jacket. The weather in Alaska can change dramatically, and you want to put layers on and take them off as needed. Bring a hat as well, as most of your body heat is lost through the head. Also bring a rain jacket because, you never know.

Have a plan but be flexible. It's best to have options along your travel route. That way, if weather or other unforeseen circumstances change a schedule, there are other things one could do, without wasting time trying to figure something else out.

Plan a two week trip at least (if possible), especially if you're visiting from the east coast. That four hour time difference can be difficult to cope with. I know it takes me at least a week to realign my body to the time difference, including one full day of just sleeping.

Alaska can be pricey so be aware of that. The shoulder seasons (May and September) are usually less expensive.

The train does not run every day in the winter, it only runs once a week. I learned this my first day in Alaska.

You may not find regular bathrooms, in some places in Alaska. But you will always find an outhouse (overheard in a public latrine – "I don't get it. It's just a hole in the ground".)

Alaska

You'll notice the scent of wood burning, and many unfinished houses up here.

Alaskans eat more ice cream than any other state.

Lastly, come and visit (or explore further), this beautiful, rugged state of Alaska, with so much to offer and beauty to behold.

If you enjoyed this book or received value from it in any way, would you be kind enough to leave a review for this book on Amazon? I would be so grateful. Thank you!

Made in the USA
San Bernardino, CA
08 December 2016